Tertullian
The Soul's Testimony

Tertullian
The Soul's Testimony

Tertullian
The Soul's Testimony

© Lighthouse Publishing 2018

Tertullian (155 – 240)

Translated by: Rev. S. Thelwall (1834 – 1922)

Revised by: A.M. Overett (b. 1960)

All rights reserved. Without limiting the rights under copyright reserved above, no part of this publication may be reproduced, stored in a retrieval system, or transmitted, in any form or by any means (electronic, mechanical, photocopying, recording or otherwise), without the prior written permission of the copyright owner of this book.

Published by
Lighthouse Christian Publishing
SAN 257-4330
5531 Dufferin Drive
Savage, Minnesota, 55378
United States of America

www.lighthousechristianpublishing.com

Tertullian

Introductory Note.

[a.d. 145–220.] When our Lord repulsed the woman of Canaan (Matt. xv. 22) with apparent harshness, he applied to her people the epithet *dogs*, with which the children of Israel had thought it piety to reproach them. When He accepted her faith and caused it to be recorded for our learning, He did something more: He reversed the curse of the Canaanite and showed that the Church was designed "for all people;" Catholic alike for all time and for all sorts and conditions of men.

Thus the North-African Church was loved before it was born: the Good Shepherd was gently leading those "that were with young." Here was the charter of those Christians to be a Church, who then were Canaanites in the land of their father Ham. It is remarkable indeed that among these pilgrims and strangers to the West the first elements of Latin Christianity come into view. Even at the close of the Second Century the Church in Rome is an inconsiderable, though prominent, member of the great confederation of Christian Churches which has its chief seats in Alexandria and Antioch, and of which the entire Literature is Greek. It is an African presbyter who takes from Latin Christendom the reproach of theological and literary barrenness and begins the great work in which, upon his foundations, Cyprian and Augustine built up, with incomparable genius, that Carthaginian School of Christian thought by which Latin Theology was dominated for centuries. It is important to note (1.) that providentially not one of these illustrious doctors died in Communion with the Roman See, pure though it was and venerable at that time; and (2.) that to the works of Augustine the Reformation in Germany and Continental Europe was largely due; while (3.) the *specialties* of the Anglican Reformation were, in like proportion, due to the writings of Tertullian and Cyprian. The hinges of great and controlling destinies for Western Europe and our own America are to be found in the period we are now approaching.

    The merest school-boy knows much of the history of Carthage, and how the North Africans became Roman citizens. How they became Christians is not so clear. A melancholy destiny has enveloped Carthage from the outset, and its glory and greatness as a Christian See were transient indeed. It blazed out all at once in Tertullian, after about a century of missionary labours had been exerted upon its creation: and having given a Minucius Felix, an Arnobius and a Lactantius to adorn the earliest period of Western Ecclesiastical learning, in addition to its nobler luminaries, it rapidly declined. At the beginning of the Third Century, at a council presided over by Agrippinus, Bishop of Carthage, there were present not less than seventy bishops of the Province. A period of cruel persecutions followed, and the African Church received a baptism of blood.

    Tertullian was born a heathen, and seems to have been educated at Rome, where he probably practiced as a jurisconsult. We may, perhaps, adopt most of the ideas of Allix, as conjecturally probable, and assign his birth to a.d. 145. He became a Christian about 185, and a presbyter about 190. The period of his strict orthodoxy very nearly expires with the century. He lived to an extreme old age, and some suppose even till a.d. 240. More probably we must adopt the date preferred by recent writers, a.d. 220.

It seems to be the fashion to treat of Tertullian as a Montanist, and only incidentally to celebrate his services to the Catholic Orthodoxy of Western Christendom. Were I his biographer I should reverse this course, as a mere act of justice, to say nothing of gratitude to a man of splendid intellect, to whom the filial spirit of Cyprian accorded the loving tribute of a disciple, and whose genius stamped itself upon the very words of Latin theology, and prepared the language for the labors of a Jerome. In creating the Vulgate, and so lifting the Western Churches into a position of intellectual equality with the East, the latter as well as St. Augustine himself were debtors to Tertullian in a degree not to be estimated by any other than the Providential Mind that inspired his brilliant career as a Christian.

In speaking of Tatian I laid the base for what I wished to say of Tertullian. Let God only be their judge; let us gratefully recognize the debt we owe to them. Let us read them, as we read the works of King Solomon. We must, indeed, approve of the discipline of the Primitive Age, which allowed of no compromises. The Church was struggling for existence, and could not permit any man to become her master. The more brilliant the intellect, the more dangerous to the poor Church were its perversions of her Testimony. Before the heathen tribunals, and in the market-places, it would not answer to let Christianity appear double tongued. The orthodoxy of the Church, not less than her children, was undergoing an ordeal of fire. It seems a miracle that her Testimony preserved its unity, and that heresy was branded as such by the instinct of the Faithful. Poor Tertullian was cut off by his own act. The weeping Church might bewail him as David mourned for Absalom, but like David, she could not give the Ark of God into other hands than those of the loyal and the true. I have set the writings of Tertullian in a natural and logical order, so as to aid the student, and to relieve him from the distractions of such an arrangement as one finds in Oehler's edition. Valuable as it is, the practical use of it is irritating and confusing. The reader of that edition may turn to the slightly differing schemes of Neander and Kaye, for a theoretical order of the works; but here he will find a classification which will aid his inquiries. He will find, first, those works which connect with the Apologists of the former volumes of this series: which illustrate the Church's position toward the outside world, the Jews as well as the Gentiles. Next come those works which contend with internal differences and heresies. And then, those which reflect the morals and manners of Christians. These are classed with some reference to their degrees of freedom from the Montanistic taint, and are followed, last of all, by the few tracts which belong to the melancholy period of his lapse, and are directed against the Church's orthodoxy.

Let it be borne in mind, that if this sad close of Tertullian's career cannot be extenuated, the later history of Latin Christianity forbids us to condemn him, in the tones which proceeded from the Virgin Church with authority, and which the law of her testimony and the instinct of self-preservation forced her to utter. Let us reflect that St. Bernard and after him the Schoolmen, whom we so deservedly honor, separated themselves far more absolutely than ever Tertullian did from the orthodoxy of Primitive Christendom. The schism which withdrew the West from Communion with the original seats of Christendom, and from Nicene Catholicity, was formidable beyond all expression, in comparison with Tertullian's entanglements with a delusion which the See of Rome itself had momentarily patronized. Since the Council of Trent, not a theologian of the Latins has been free from organic heresies, compared with which the fanaticism of our author was a trifling aberration. Since the late Council of the Vatican, essential Montanism has become organized in the Latin Churches: for what are the new revelations and oracles of the pontiff but the *deliria* of another claimant to the voice and inspiration of the Paraclete? Poor Tertullian! The sad influences of his decline and folly have been fatally felt in all the subsequent history of the West, but, surely subscribers to the Modern Creed of the Vatican have reason to "speak gently of *their father's* fall." To Döllinger, with the "Old Catholic" remnant only, is left the right to name the Montanists heretics, or to upbraid Tertullian as a lapser from Catholicity.

From Dr. Holmes, I append the following Introductory Notice:

(I.) Quintus Septimius Florens Tertullianus, as our author is called in the mss. of his works, is thus noticed by Jerome in his *Catalogus Scriptorum Ecclesiasticorum:* "Tertullian, a presbyter, the first Latin writer after Victor and Apollonius, was a native of the province of Africa and city of Carthage, the son of a proconsular centurion: he was a man of a sharp and vehement temper, flourished under Severus and Antoninus Caracalla, and wrote numerous works, which (as they are generally known) I think it unnecessary to particularize. I saw at Concordia, in Italy, an old man named Paulus. He said that when young he had met at Rome with an aged amanuensis of the blessed Cyprian, who told him that Cyprian never passed a day without reading some portion of Tertullian's works, and used frequently to say, *Give me my master*, meaning Tertullian. After remaining a presbyter of the church until he had attained the middle age of life, Tertullian was, by the envy and contumelious treatment of the Roman clergy, driven to embrace the opinions of Montanus, which he has mentioned in several of his works under the title of the New Prophecy....He is reported to have lived to a very advanced age, and to have composed many other works which are not extant." We add Bishop Kaye's notes on this extract, in an abridged shape: "The correctness of some parts of this account has been questioned. Doubts have been entertained whether Tertullian was a presbyter, although these have solely arisen from Roman Catholic objections to a married priesthood; for it is certain that he was married, there being among his works two treatises addressed to his wife....Another question has been raised respecting the place where Tertullian officiated as a presbyter—whether at Carthage or at Rome. That he at one time resided at Carthage may be inferred from Jerome's statement, and is rendered certain by several passages of his own writings. Allix supposes that the notion of his having been a presbyter of the Roman Church owed its rise to what Jerome said of the envy and abuse of the Roman clergy impelling him to espouse the party of Montanus. Optatus, and the author of the work *de Hæresibus*, which Sirmond edited under the title of Prædestinatus, expressly call him a Carthaginian presbyter. Semler, however, in a dissertation inserted in his edition of Tertullian's works, contends that he was a presbyter of the Roman Church. Eusebius tells us that he was accurately acquainted with the Roman laws, and on other accounts a distinguished person at Rome. Tertullian displays, moreover, a knowledge of the proceedings of the Roman Church with respect to Marcion and Valentinus, who were once members of it, which could scarcely have been obtained by one who had not himself been numbered amongst its presbyters Semler admits that, after Tertullian seceded from the church, he left and returned to Carthage. Jerome does not inform us whether Tertullian was born of Christian parents, or was converted to Christianity. There are passages in his writings which seem to imply that he had been a Gentile; yet he may perhaps mean to describe, not his own condition, but that of Gentiles in general, before their conversion. Allix and the majority of commentators understand them literally, as well as some other passages in which he speaks of his own infirmities and sinfulness. His writings show that he flourished at the period specified by Jerome—that is, during the reigns of Severus and Antoninus Caracalla, or between the years a.d. 193 and 216; but they supply no precise information respecting the date of his birth, or any of the principal occurrences of his life. Allix places his birth about 145 or 150; his conversion to Christianity about a.d. 185; his marriage about 186; his admission to the priesthood about 192; his adoption of the opinions of Montanus about 199; and his death about a.d. 220.

But these dates, it must be understood, rest entirely on conjecture."

(II.) Tertullian's work against Marcion, as it happens, is, *as to its date*, the best authenticated—perhaps the only well authenticated—particular connected with the author's life.
He himself mentions the fifteenth year of the reign of Severus as the time when he was writing the work: "Ad xv. jam Severi imperatoris." This agrees with Jerome's Chronicle, where occurs this note: "Anno 2223 Severi xv° Tertullianus...celebratur." This year is assigned to the year of our Lord 207; but notwithstanding the certainty of this date, it is far from clear that it describes more than the time of the publication of *the first book*. On the contrary, it is nearly certain that the other books, although connected manifestly enough in the author's argument and purpose (compare the initial and the final chapters of the several books), were yet issued at separate times. Noesselt shows that between the Book i. and Books ii.–iv. Tertullian issued his *De Præscript. Hæret.*, and previous to Book v. he published his tracts, *De Carne Christi* and *De Resurrectione Carnis*. After giving the incontestable date of the xv. of Severus for the first book, he says it is a mistake to suppose that the other books were published with it. He adds: "Although we cannot undertake to determine whether Tertullian issued his Books ii., iii., iv., against Marcion, together or separately, or in what year, we yet venture to affirm that Book v. appeared apart from the rest. For the tract *De Resurr. Carnis* appears from its second chapter to have been published after the tract *De Carne Christi*, in which latter work (chap. vii.) he quotes a passage from the fourth book against Marcion. But in his Book v. against Marcion (chap. x.), he refers to his work *De Resurr. Carnis*; which circumstance makes it evident that Tertullian published his Book v. at a different time from his Book iv. In his Book i. he announces his intention (chap. i.) of some time or other completing his tract *De Præscript. Hæret.*, but in his book *De Carne Christi* (chap. ii.), he mentions how he had completed

it,—a conclusive proof that his Book i. against Marcion preceded the other books."

(III.) Respecting Marcion himself, the most formidable heretic who had as yet opposed revealed truth, enough will turn up in this treatise, with the notes which we have added in explanation, to satisfy the reader. It will, however, be convenient to give here a few introductory particulars of him. Tertullian mentions Marcion as being, with Valentinus, in communion with the Church at Rome, "under the episcopate of the blessed Eleutherus." He goes on to charge them with "ever-restless curiosity, with which they infected even the brethren;" and informs us that they were more than once put out of communion—"Marcion, indeed, with the 200 sesterces which he brought into the church." He goes on to say, that "being at last condemned to the banishment of a perpetual separation, they sowed abroad the poisons of their doctrines. Afterwards, when Marcion, having professed penitence, agreed to the terms offered to him, that he should receive reconciliation on condition that he brought back to the church the rest also, whom he had trained up for perdition, he was prevented by death." He was a native of Sinope in Pontus, of which city, according to an account preserved by Epiphanius, which, however, is somewhat doubtful, his father was bishop, and of high character both for his orthodoxy and exemplary practice. He came to Rome soon after the death of Hyginus, probably about a.d. 141 or 142; and soon after his arrival he adopted the heresy of Cerdon.

(IV.) It is an interesting question as to what edition of the Holy Scriptures Tertullian used in his very copious quotations. It may at once be asserted that he did not cite from the Hebrew, although some writers have claimed for him, among his varied learning, a knowledge of the sacred language. Bp. Kaye observes, page 61, n. 1, that "he sometimes speaks as if he was acquainted with Hebrew," and refers to the *Anti-Marcion* iv. 39, the *Adv. Praxeam* v., and the *Adv. Judæos* ix. Be this as it may, it is manifest that Tertullian's Scripture

passages never resemble the Hebrew, but in nearly every instance the Septuagint, whenever, as is most frequently the case, that version differs from the original. In the New Testament there is, as might be expected, a tolerably close conformity to the Greek. There is, however, it must be allowed, a sufficiently frequent variation from the letter of both the Greek Testaments to justify Semler's suspicion that Tertullian always quoted from the old Latin version, whatever that might have been, which was current in the African church in the second and third centuries. The most valuable part of Semler's *Dissertatio de varia et incerta indole Librorum Q. S. F. Tertulliani* is his investigation of this very point. In section iv. he endeavors to prove this proposition: "Hic scriptor non in manibus habuit Græcos libros sacros;" and he states his conclusion thus: "Certissimum est nec Tertullianum nec Cyprianum nec ullum scriptorem e Latinis illis ecclesiasticis provocare unquam ad Græcorum librorum auctoritatem
si vel maxime obscura aut contraria lectio occurreret;" and again: "Ex his satis certum est, Latinos satis diu secutos fuisse auctoritatem suorum librorum adversus Græcos, nec
concessisse nisi serius, cum Augustini et Hieronymi nova auctoritas juvare videretur." It is not ignorance of Greek which is imputed to Tertullian, for he is said to have well understood that language, and even to have composed in it. He probably followed the Latin, as writers now usually quote the authorized English, as being current and best known among their readers. Independent feeling, also, would have weight with such a temper as Tertullian's, to say nothing of the suspicion which largely prevailed in the African branch of the Latin church, that the Greek copies of the Scriptures were much corrupted by the heretics, who were chiefly, if not wholly, Greeks or Greek-speaking persons.

(V.) Whatever perverting effect Tertullian's secession to the sect of Montanus may have had on his judgment in his latest writings, it did not vitiate the work against Marcion. With a few trivial exceptions, this treatise may be read by the strictest Catholic without any feeling of annoyance. His lapse to Montanism is set down conjecturally as having taken place a.d. 199. Jerome, we have seen, attributed the event to his quarrel with the Roman clergy, but this is at least doubtful; nor must it be forgotten that Tertullian's mind seems to have been peculiarly suited by nature to adopt the mystical notions and ascetic principles of Montanus. It is satisfactory to find that, on the whole, "the authority of Tertullian," as the learned Dr. Burton says, "upon great points of doctrine is considered to be little, if at all, affected by his becoming a Montanist." (*Lectures on Eccl. Hist.* vol. ii. p. 234.) Besides the different works which are expressly mentioned in the notes of this volume, recourse has been had by the translator to Dupin's *Hist. Eccl. Writers* (trans.), vol. i. pp. 69–86; Tillemont's *Mèmoires Hist. Eccl.* iii. 85–103; Dr. Smith's *Greek and Roman Biography*, articles "Marcion" and "Tertullian;" Schaff's article, in Herzog's *Cyclopædia*, on "Tertullian;" Munter's *Primordia Eccl. Africanæ*, pp. 118–150; Robertson's *Church Hist.* vol. i. pp. 70–77; Dr. P. Schaff's *Hist. of Christian Church* (New York, 1859, pp. 511–519), and Archdeacon Evans' *Biography of the Early Church*, vol. i. (Lives of "Marcion," pp. 93–122, and "Tertullian," pp. 325–363). This last work, though of a popular cast, shows a good deal of research and learning, expressed in the pleasant style of the once popular author of *The Rectory of Vale Head*. The translator has mentioned these works, because they are all quite accessible to the general reader, and will give him adequate information concerning the subject treated in the present volume.

To this introduction of Dr. Holmes must be added that of Mr. Thelwall, the translator of the Third volume in the Edinburgh Series, as follows:

To arrange chronologically the works (especially if numerous) of an author whose own date is known with tolerable precision, is not always or necessarily easy: witness the controversies as to the succession of St. Paul's epistles. To do this in the case of an author whose own date is itself a matter of controversy may therefore be reasonably expected to be still less so; and such is the predicament of him who attempts to perform this task for Tertullian. I propose to give a specimen or two of the difficulties with which the task is beset; and then to lay before the reader briefly a summary of the results at which eminent scholars, who have devoted much time and thought to the subject, have arrived. Such a course, I think, will at once afford him means of judging of the absolute impossibility of arriving at definite certainty in the matter; and induce him to excuse me if I prefer furnishing him with materials from which to deduce his own conclusions, rather than venturing on an *ex cathedra* decision on so doubtful a subject.

 I. The book, as Dr. Holmes has reminded us, of the date of which we seem to have the surest evidence, is *Adv. Marc.* i. This book was in course of writing, as its author himself (c. 15) tells us, "in the fifteenth year of the empire of Severus." Now this date would be clear if there were no doubt as to which year of our era corresponds to Tertullian's fifteenth of Severus. Pamelius, however, says Dr. Holmes, makes it a.d. 208; Clinton, (whose authority is more recent and better,) 207.

 2. Another book which promises to give some clue to its date is the *de Pallio*. The writer uses these phrases: "præsentis imperii *triplex virtus*;" "Deo *tot Augustis in unum* favente;" which show that there were at the time three persons unitedly bearing the title *Augusti*—not *Cæsares* only, but the still higher *Augusti*;—while the remainder of that context, as well as the opening of c. 1, indicates a time of peace of some considerable duration; a time of plenty; and a time during and previous to which great changes had taken place in the general aspect of the Roman Empire, and some particular traitor had been discovered and frustrated. Such a combination of circumstances might seem to fix the date with some degree of assurance. But unhappily, as Kaye reminds us, commentators cannot agree as to who the three Augusti are. Some say

Severus, Caracalla, and *Albinus*; some say Severus, Caracalla, and *Geta*. Hence we have a difference of some twelve years or thereabouts in the computations. For Albinus was defeated by Severus in person, and fell by his own hand, in a.d. 197; and Geta, Severus' second son, brother of Caracalla, was not associated by his father with himself and his other son as *Augustus* until a.d. 208, though he had received the title of *Cæsar* ten years before, in the same year in which *Caracalla* had received that of Augustus. For my own part, I may perhaps be allowed to say that I should incline to agree, like Salmasius, with those who assign the later date. The limits of the present Introduction forbid my entering at large into my reasons for so doing. I am, however, supported in it by the authority of Neander. In one point, though, I should hesitate to agree with Oehler, who appears to follow Salmasius and others herein,— namely, in understanding the expression "et cacto et rubo subdolæ familiaritatis convulso" of *Albinus*. It seems to me the words might with more propriety be applied to *Plautianus*; and that in the word "familiaritatis" we may see (after Tertullian's fashion) a play upon the meaning, with a reference not only to the long-standing but mischievous *intimacy* which existed between Severus and his countryman (perhaps fellow-townsman) Plautianus, who for his harshness and cruelty is fitly compared to the prickly *cactus*. He alludes likewise to the alliance which this ambitious prætorian præfect had contrived to contract with the *family* of the emperor, by the marriage of his daughter Plautilla to Caracalla,—an event which, as it turned out, led to his own death. Thus in the "*rubo*" there may be a reference to the ambitious and conceited "bramble" of Jotham's parable, and perhaps, too, to the "thistle" of Jehoash's. If this be so, the date would be at least approximately fixed, as Plautianus did not marry his daughter to Caracalla till a.d. 203, and was himself put to death in the following year, 204, while Geta, as we have seen, was made Augustus in 208.

3. The date of the *Apology*, however, is perhaps at once the most contested, and the most strikingly illustrative of the difficulties to which allusion has been made. It is not surprising that its date *should* have been more disputed than that of other pieces, inasmuch as it is the best known, and (for some reasons) the most interesting and famous, of all our author's productions. In fact, the dates assigned to it by different authorities vary from Mosheim's 198 to that suggested by the very learned Allix, who assigns it to 217.

4. Once more. In the tract *de Monogamia* (c. 3) the author says that since the date of St. Paul's first Epistle to the Corinthians "about 160 years had elapsed." Here, again, did we only know with certainty the precise date of that epistle, we could ascertain "about" the date of the tract. But (a) the date of the epistle is itself variously given, Burton giving it as early as a.d. 52, Michaelis and Mill as late as 57; and (b) Tertullian only says, "Armis *circiter* clx. exinde productis;" while the way in which, in the *ad Natt.*, within the short space of three chapters, he states first that 250, and then (in c. 9) that 300, years had not elapsed since the rise of the Christian name, leads us to think that here again he only desires to speak in round numbers, meaning perhaps *more* than 150, but *less* than 170.

These specimens must suffice, though it might be easy to add to them. There is, however, another classification of our author's writings which has been attempted. Finding the haplessness of strict chronological accuracy, commentators have seized on the idea that peradventure there might be found at all events some internal marks by which to determine which of them were written before, which after, the writer's secession to Montanism. It may be confessed that this attempt has been somewhat more successful than the other. Yet even here there are two formidable obstacles standing in our way. The first and greatest is, that the natural temper of Tertullian was from the first so akin to the spirit of Montanism, that, unless there occur distinct allusions to the "New Prophecy," or expressions specially connected with Montanistic phraseology, the *general tone* of any treatise is not a very safe guide. The second is, that the subject-matter of some of the treatises is not such as to afford much scope for the introduction of the peculiarities of a sect which professed to differ in discipline only, not doctrine, from the church at large.

Still the result of this classification seems to show one important feature of agreement between commentators, however they may differ upon details; and that is, that considerably the larger part of our author's rather voluminous productions must have been subsequent to his lamented secession. I think the best way to give the reader means for forming his own judgment will be, as I have said, to lay before him in parallel columns a tabular view of the disposition of the books by Dr. Neander and Bishop Kaye. These two modern writers, having given particular care to the subject, bringing to bear upon it all the advantages derived from wide reading, eminent abilities, and a diligent study of the works of preceding writers on the same questions, have a special right to be heard upon the matter in hand; and I think, if I may be allowed to say so, that, for calm judgment, and minute acquaintance with his author, I shall not be accused of undue partiality if I express my opinion that, as far as my own observation goes, the palm must be awarded to the Bishop. In this view I am supported by the fact that the accomplished Professor Ramsay, follows Dr. Kaye's arrangement. I premise that Dr. Neander adopts a threefold division, into:

1. Writings which were occasioned by the relation of the Christians to the heathen, and refer to their vindication of Christianity against the heathen; attacks on heathenism; the sufferings and conduct of Christians under persecution; and the intercourse of Christians with heathens:

2. Writings which relate to Christian and church life, and to ecclesiastical discipline:

3. The dogmatic and dogmatico-controversial treatises.

And under each head he subdivides into:

a. Pre-Montanist writings; b. Post-Montanist writings: thus leaving no room for what Kaye calls "works respecting which nothing certain can be pronounced." For the sake of clearness, this order has not been followed in the table. On the other side, it will be seen that Dr. Kaye, while not assuming to speak with more than a reasonable probability, is careful so to arrange the treatises under each head as to show the order, so far as it is discoverable, in which the books under that head were published; i.e., if one book is quoted in another book, the book so quoted, if distinctly referred to as already before the world, is plainly anterior to that in which it is quoted. Thus, then, have:

Neander.
I. *Pre-Montanist.*
1. De Poenitentia.
2. De Oratione.
3. De Baptismo.
4. Ad Uxorem i.
5. Ad Uxorem ii.
6. Ad Martyres.
7. De Patientia.
8. De Spectaculis.
9. De Idololatria.
10. 11. Ad Nationes i. ii.
12. Apologeticus.
13. De Testimonio Animæ.
14. De Præscr. Hæreticorum.
15. De Cult. Fem. i.
16. De Cult. Fem. ii.
II. *Montanist.*
17–21. Adv. Marc. i. ii. iii. iv. v.
22. De Anima.
23. De Carne Christi.
24. De Res. Carn.
25. De Cor. Mil.

26. De Virg. Vel.
27. De Ex. Cast.
28. De Monog.
29. De Jejuniis.
30. De Pudicitia.
31. De Pallio.
32. Scorpiace.
33. Ad Scapulam.
34. Adv. Valentinianos.
35. Adv. Hermogenem.
36. Adv. Praxeam.
37. Adv. Judæos.
38. De Fuga in Persecutione.
Kaye.
I. *Pre-Montanist* (probably).
1. De Poenitentia.
2. De Oratione.
3. De Baptismo.
4. Ad Uxorem i.
5. Ad Uxorem ii.
6. Ad Martyres.
7. De Patientia.
8. Adv. Judæos.
9. De Præscr. Hæreticorum.
II. *Montanist* (certainly).
10. Adv. Marc. i.
11. Adv. Marc. ii.
12. De Anima.
13. Adv. Marc. iii.
14. Adv. Marc. iv.
15. De Carne Christi.
16. De Resurrectione Carnis.
17. Adv. Marc. v.
18. Adv. Praxeam.
19. Scorpiace.
20. De Corona Militis.

21. De Virginibus Velandis.
22. De Exhortatione Castitatis.
23. De Fuga in Persecutione.
24. De Monogamia.
25. De Jejuniis.
26. De Pudicitia.
III. *Montanist* (probably).
27. Adv. Valentinianos.
28. Ad Scapulam.
29. De Spectaculis.
30. De Idololatria.
31. De Cultu Feminarum i.
32. De Cultu Feminarum ii.
IV. *Works respecting which nothing certain can be pronounced.*
33. The Apology.
34. Ad Nationes i.
35. Ad Nationes ii.
36. De Testimonio Animæ.
37. De Pallio.
38. Adv. Hermogenem.

  A comparison of these two lists will show that the difference between the two great authorities is, as Kaye remarks, "not great; and with respect to some of the tracts on which we differ, the learned author expresses himself with great diffidence." The main difference, in fact, is that which affects two tracts upon kindred subjects, the *de Spectaculis*, and *Idololatria*, the *de Cultu Feminarum* (a subject akin to the other two), and the *adv. Judæos*. With reference to all these, except the last, to which I believe the Archdeacon does not once refer, the Bishop's opinion appears to have the support of Archdeacon Evans, whose learned and interesting essay, referred to in the note, appears in a volume published in 1837. Dr. Kaye's Lectures, on which his book is founded, were delivered in 1825. Of the date of his first edition I am not aware. Dr. Neander's *Antignostikus* also first appeared in 1825.

The Soul's Testimony

The preface to his second edition bears date July 1, 1849. As to the *adv. Judæos,* I confess I agree with Neander in thinking that, at all events from the beginning of c. 9, it is spurious. If it be urged that Jerome expressly quotes it as Tertullian's, I reply, Jerome so quotes it, I believe, when he is expounding *Daniel.* Now all that the *adv. Jud.* has to say about *Daniel* ends with the end of c. 8. It is therefore quite compatible with the fact thus stated to recognize the earlier half of the book as genuine, and to reject the rest, beginning, as it happens, just after the eighth chapter, as spurious. Perhaps Dr. Neander's Jewish birth and training peculiarly fit him to be heard on this question. Nor do I think Professor Ramsay (in the article above alluded to) has quite seen the force of Kaye's own remarks on Neander. What he does say is equally creditable to his candor and his accuracy; namely: "The instances alleged by Dr. Neander, in proof of this position, are undoubtedly very remarkable; but if the concluding chapters of the tract are spurious, no ground seems to be left for asserting that the genuine portion was posterior to the third Book against Marcion,—and none, consequently, for asserting that it was written by a Montanist." With which remark I must draw these observations on the genuine extant works of Tertullian to a close.

The next point to which a brief reference must be made is the *lost works* of Tertullian, lists of these are given both by Oehler and by Kaye, viz.:

1. A Book on Aaron's Robes: mentioned by Jerome, Epist. 128, *ad Fabiolam de Veste Sacerdotali* (tom. ii. p. 586, Opp. ed. Bened.).

2. A Book on the Superstition of the Age.

3. A Book on the Submission of the Soul.

4. A Book on the Flesh and the Soul.

Nos. 2, 3, and 4 are known only by their titles, which are found in the Index to Tertullian's works given in the *Codex Agobardi*; but the tracts themselves are not extant in the ms., which appears to have once contained—

5. A Book on Paradise, named in the Index, and referred to in *de Anima* 55, *adv. Marc.* iii. 12; and

6. A Book on the Hope of the Faithful: also named in the Index, and referred to *adv. Marc.* iii. 24; and by Jerome in his account of Papias, and on Ezek. xxxvi.; and by Gennadius of Marseilles.

7. Six Books on Ecstasy, with a seventh in reply to Apollonius: see Jerome. See, too, J. A. Fabricius on the words of the unknown author whom the Jesuit Sirmond edited under the name *Prædestinatus*; who gathers thence that "Soter, pope of the City, and Apollonius, bishop of the Ephesians, wrote a book against the Montanists; *in reply to whom* Tertullian, a Carthaginian presbyter, wrote." J. Pamelius thinks these seven books were originally published *in Greek.*

8. A Book in reply to the Apellesites (i.e. the followers of Apelles): referred to in *de Carne Christi,* c. 8.

9. A Book on the Origin of the Soul, in reply to Hermogenes: referred to in *de Anima,* cc. 1, 3, 22, 24.

10. A Book on Fate: referred to by Fulgentius Planciades, p. 562, Merc.; also referred to as either written, or intended to be written, by Tertullian himself, *de Anima,* c. 20. Jerome states that there was extant, or had been extant, a book on Fate under the name of Minucius Felix, written indeed by a perspicuous author, but not in the style of Minucius Felix. This, Pamelius judged, should perhaps be rather ascribed to Tertullian.

11. A Book on the Trinity. Jerome says: "Novatian wrote....a large volume on the Trinity, *as if making an epitome of a work of Tertullian's, which most men not knowing regard it as Cyprian's.*" Novatian's book stood in Tertullian's name in the mss. of J. Gangneius, who was the first to edit it; in a Malmesbury ms. which Sig. Gelenius used; and in others.

12. A Book addressed to a Philosophic Friend on the Straits of Matrimony. Both Kaye and Oehler are in doubt whether Jerome's words, by which some have been led to conclude that Tertullian wrote some book or books on this and kindred subjects, really imply as much, or whether they may

not refer merely to those tracts and passages in his extant writings which touch upon such matters. Kaye hesitates to think that the "Book to a Philosophic Friend" is the same as the *de Exhortatione Castitatis*, because Jerome says Tertullian wrote on the subject of celibacy *"in his youth;"* but as Cave takes what Jerome elsewhere says of Tertullian's leaving the Church *"about the middle of his age"* to mean his *spiritual age*, the same sense might attach to his words here too, and thus obviate the Bishop's difficulty.

There are some other works which have been attributed to Tertullian—on Circumcision; on Animals Clean and Unclean; on the truth that God is a Judge—which Oehler likewise rejects, believing that the expressions of Jerome refer only to passages in the *Anti-Marcion* and other extant works. To Novatian Jerome does ascribe a distinct work on Circumcision, and this may (comp. 11, just above) have given rise to the view that Tertullian had written one also.

There were, moreover, three treatises at least written by Tertullian *in Greek*. They are:

1. A Book on Public Shows. See *de Cor.* c. 6.
2. A Book on Baptism. See *de Bapt.* c. 15.
3. A Book on the Veiling of Virgins. See de *V. V.* c. 1.

Oehler adds that J. Pamelius, in his epistle dedicatory to Philip II. of Spain, makes mention of a *Greek copy* of Tertullian in the library of that king. This report, however, since nothing has ever been seen or heard of the said copy from that time, Oehler judges to be erroneous.

It remains briefly to notice the confessedly spurious works which the editions of Tertullian generally have appended to them. With these Kaye does not deal. The fragment, *adv. omnes Hæreses*, Oehler attributes to Victorinus Petavionensis, i.e., Victorinus bishop of Pettaw, on the Drave, in Austrian Styria. It was once thought he ought to be called *Pictaviensis*, i.e. of *Poictiers*; but John Launoy has shown this to be an error. Victorinus is said by Jerome to have "understood Greek better than Latin; hence his works are excellent for the sense, but mean as to the style." Cave believes him to have been a Greek by birth. Cassiodorus states him to have been once a professor of rhetoric. Jerome's statement agrees with the style of the tract in question; and Jerome distinctly says Victorinus did write *adversus omnes Hæreses*. Allix leaves the question of its authorship quite uncertain. If Victorinus be the author, the book falls clearly within the Ante-Nicene period; for Victorinus fell a martyr in the Diocletian persecution, probably about a.d. 303.

The next fragment—"Of the Execrable Gods of the Heathens"—is of quite uncertain authorship. Oehler would attribute it "to some declaimer not quite ignorant of Tertullian's writings," but certainly not to Tertullian himself.

Lastly we come to the metrical fragments. Concerning these, it is perhaps impossible to assign them to their rightful owners. Oehler has not troubled himself much about them; but he seems to regard the *Jonah* as worthy of more regard than the rest, for he seems to have intended giving more labor to its editing at some future time. Whether he has ever done so, or given us his German version of Tertullian's own works, which, "si Deus adjuverit," he distinctly promises in his preface, I do not know. Perhaps the best thing to be done under the circumstances is to give the judgment of the learned Peter Allix. It may be premised that by the celebrated George Fabricius—who published his great work, *Poetarum Veterum Ecclesiasticorum Opera Christiana*, etc., in 1564—the *Five Books in Reply to Marcion*, and the *Judgment of the Lord*, are ascribed to Tertullian, the *Genesis* and *Sodom* to Cyprian.
Pamelius likewise seems to have ascribed the *Five Books*, the *Jonah*, and the *Sodom* to Tertullian; and according to Lardner, Bishop Bull likewise attributed the *Five Books* to him. They have been generally ascribed to the Victorinus above mentioned. Tillemont, among others, thinks they may well enough be his. Rigaltius is content to demonstrate that they are not Tertullian's, but leaves the real authorship without attempting to decide it. Of the others the same eminent critic says, "They seem to have been written at Carthage, at an age

21

not far removed from Tertullian's." Allix, after observing that Pamelius is inconsistent with himself in attributing the *Genesis* and *Sodom* at one time to Tertullian, at another to
Cyprian, rejects both views equally, and assigns the Genesis with some confidence to Salvian, a presbyter of Marseilles, whose "floruit" Cave gives *cir*. 440, a contemporary of Gennadius, and a copious author. To this it is, Allix thinks, that Gennadius alludes in his *Catalogue of Illustrious Men*, c. 77.

The *Judgment of the Lord* Allix ascribes to one Verecundus, an African bishop, whose date he finds it difficult to decide exactly. He refers to two of the name: one Bishop of Tunis, whom Victor of Tunis in his chronicle mentions as having died in exile at Chalcedon a.d. 552; the other Bishop of Noba, who visited Carthage with many others a.d. 482, at the summons of King Huneric, to answer there for their faith;— and would ascribe the poem to the former, thinking that he finds an allusion to it in the article upon that Verecundus in the *de Viris Illustribus* of Isidore of Seville. Oehler agrees with him. The *Five Books* Allix seems to hint may be attributed to some imitator of the Victorinus of Pettaw named above.
Oehler attributes them rather to one Victorinus, or Victor, of Marseilles, a rhetorician, who died a.d. 450. He appears in G. Fabricius as Claudius Marius Victorinus, writer of a *Commentary on Genesis*, and an epistle *ad Salomonem Abbata*, both in verse, and of some considerable length.

The Soul's Testimony.

Chapter I.

If, with the object of convicting the rivals and persecutors of Christian truth, from their own authorities, of the crime of at once being untrue to themselves and doing injustice to us, one is bent on gathering testimonies in its favor from the writings of the philosophers, or the poets, or other masters of this world's learning and wisdom, he has need of a most inquisitive spirit, and a still greater memory to carry out the research. Indeed, some of our people, who still continued their inquisitive labors in ancient literature, and still occupied memory with it, have published works we have in our hands of this very sort; works in which they relate and attest the nature and origin of their traditions, and the grounds on which opinions rest, and from which it may be seen at once that we have embraced nothing new or monstrous—nothing for which we cannot claim the support of ordinary and well-known writings, whether in ejecting error from our creed, or admitting truth into it. But the unbelieving hardness of the human heart leads them to slight even their own teachers, otherwise approved and in high renown, whenever they touch upon arguments which are used in defense of Christianity. Then the poets are fools, when they describe the gods with human passions and stories; then the philosophers are without reason, when they knock at the gates of truth. He will thus far be reckoned a wise and sagacious man who has gone the length of uttering sentiments that are almost Christian; while if, in a mere affectation of judgment and wisdom, he sets himself to reject their ceremonies, or to convicting the world of its sin, he is sure to be branded as a Christian. We will have nothing, then, to do with the literature and the teaching, perverted in its best results, which is believed in its errors rather than its truth. We shall lay no stress on it, if some of their authors have declared that there is one God, and one God only. Nay, let it be granted that there is nothing in heathen writers which a Christian approves, that it may be put out of his power to utter a single word of reproach. For all are not familiar with their teachings; and those who are, have no assurance in regard to their truth. Far less do men assent to our writings, to which no one comes for guidance unless he is already a Christian. I call in a new testimony, yea, one which is better known than all literature, more discussed than all doctrine, more public than all publications, greater than the whole man—I mean all which is man's. Stand forth, O soul, whether thou art a divine and eternal substance, as most philosophers believe if it be so, thou wilt be the less likely to lie,—or whether thou art the very opposite of divine, because indeed a mortal thing, as Epicurus alone thinks—in that case there will be the less temptation for thee to speak falsely in this case: whether thou art received from heaven, or sprung from earth; whether thou art formed of numbers, or of atoms; whether thine existence begins with that of the body, or thou art put into it at a later stage; from whatever source, and in whatever way, thou makest man a rational being, in the highest degree capable of thought and knowledge,—stand forth and give thy witness. But I call thee not as when, fashioned in schools, trained in libraries, fed in Attic academies and porticoes, thou belchest wisdom. I address thee simple, rude, uncultured and untaught, such as they have thee who have thee only; that very thing of the road, the street, the work-shop, wholly. I want thine inexperience, since in thy small experience no one feels any confidence. I demand of thee the things thou bringest with thee into man, which thou knowest either from thyself, or from thine author, whoever he may be. Thou art not, as I well know, Christian; for a man becomes a Christian, he is not born one. Yet Christians earnestly press thee for a testimony; they press thee, though an alien, to bear witness against thy friends, that they may be put to shame before thee, for hating and mocking us on account of things which convict thee as an accessory.

Chapter II.

We give offence by proclaiming that there is one God, to whom the name of God alone belongs, from whom all things come, and who is Lord of the whole universe. Bear thy testimony, if thou knowest this to be the truth; for openly and with a perfect liberty, such as we do not possess, we hear thee both in private and in public exclaim, "Which may God grant," and, "If God so will." By expressions such as these thou declarest that there is one who is distinctively God, and thou confessest that all power belongs to him to whose will, as Sovereign, thou dost look. At the same time, too, thou deniest any others to be truly gods, in calling them by their own names of Saturn, Jupiter, Mars, Minerva; for thou affirmest Him to be God alone to whom thou givest no other name than God; and though thou sometimes callest these others gods, thou plainly usest the designation as one which does not really belong to them, but is, so to speak, a borrowed one. Nor is the nature of the God we declare unknown to thee: "God is good, God does good," thou art wont to say; plainly suggesting further, "But man is evil." In asserting an antithetic proposition, thou, in a sort of indirect and figurative way, reproachest man with his wickedness in departing from a God so good. So, again, as among us, as belonging to the God of benignity and goodness, "Blessing" is a most sacred act in our religion and our life, thou too sayest as readily as a Christian needs, "God bless thee;" and when thou turnest the blessing of God into a curse, in like manner thy very words confess with us that His power over us is absolute and entire. There are some who, though they do not deny the existence of God, hold withal that He is neither Searcher, nor Ruler, nor Judge; treating with especial disdain those of us who go over to Christ out of fear of a coming judgment, as they think, honoring God in freeing Him from the cares of keeping watch, and the trouble of taking note,—not even regarding Him as capable of anger. For if God, they say, gets angry, then He is susceptible of corruption and passion;

The Soul's Testimony

but that of which passion and corruption can be affirmed may also perish, which God cannot do. But these very persons elsewhere, confessing that the soul is divine, and bestowed on us by God, stumble against a testimony of the soul itself, which affords an answer to these views. For if either divine or God-given, it doubtless knows its giver; and if it knows Him, it undoubtedly fears Him too, and especially as having been by Him endowed so amply. Has it no fear of Him whose favor it is so desirous to possess, and whose anger it is so anxious to avoid? Whence, then, the soul's natural fear of God, if God cannot be angry? How is there any dread of Him whom nothing offends? What is feared but anger? Whence comes anger, but from observing what is done? What leads to watchful oversight, but judgment in prospect? Whence is judgment, but from power? To whom does supreme authority and power belong, but to God alone? So thou art always ready, O soul, from thine own knowledge, nobody casting scorn upon thee, and no one preventing, to exclaim, "God sees all," and "I commend thee to God," and "May God repay," and "God shall judge between us." How happens this, since thou art not Christian? How is it that, even with the garland of Ceres on the brow, wrapped in the purple cloak of Saturn, wearing the white robe of the goddess Isis, thou invokest God as judge? Standing under the statue of Æsculapius, adorning the brazen image of Juno, arraying the helmet of Minerva with dusky figures, thou never thinkest of appealing to any of these deities. In thine own forum thou appealest to a God who is elsewhere; thou permittest honor to be rendered in thy temples to a foreign god. Oh, striking testimony to truth, which in the very midst of demons obtains a witness for us Christians!

Chapter III.

But when we say that there are demons—as though, in the simple fact that we alone expel them from the men's bodies, we did not also prove their existence—some disciple of

Chrysippus begins to curl the lip. Yet thy curses sufficiently attest that there are such beings, and that they are objects of thy strong dislike. As what comes to thee as a fit expression of thy strong hatred of him, thou callest the man a dæmon who annoys thee with his filthiness, or malice, or insolence, or any other vice which we ascribe to evil spirits. In expressing vexation, contempt, or abhorrence, thou hast Satan constantly upon thy lips; the very same we hold to be the angel of evil, the source of error, the corrupter of the whole world, by whom in the beginning man was entrapped into breaking the commandment of God. And (the man) being given over to death on account of his sin, the entire human race, tainted in their descent from him, were made a channel for transmitting his condemnation. Thou seest, then, thy destroyer; and though he is fully known only to Christians, or to whatever sect confesses the Lord, yet, even thou hast some acquaintance with him while yet thou abhorrest him!

Chapter IV.

Even now, as the matter refers to thy opinion on a point the more closely belonging to thee, in so far as it bears on thy personal well-being, we maintain that after life has passed away thou still remainest in existence, and lookest forward to a day of judgment, and according to thy deserts art assigned to misery or bliss, in either way of it forever; that, to be capable of this, thy former substance must needs return to thee, the matter and the memory of the very same human being: for neither good nor evil couldst thou feel if thou wert not endowed again with that sensitive bodily organization, and there would be no grounds for judgment without the presentation of the very person to whom the sufferings of judgment were due. That Christian view, though much nobler than the Pythagorean, as it does not transfer thee into beasts; though more complete than the Platonic, since it endows thee again with a body; though more worthy of honor than the Epicurean, as it preserves thee from annihilation,—yet, because of the name connected with it, it is held to be nothing but vanity and folly, and, as it is called, a mere presumption. But we are not ashamed of ourselves if our presumption is found to have thy support. Well, in the first place, when thou speakest of one who is dead, thou sayest of him, "Poor man"—poor, surely, not because he has been taken from the good of life, but because he has been given over to punishment and condemnation. But at another time thou speakest of the dead as free from trouble; thou professes to think life a burden, and death a blessing. Thou art wont, too, to speak of the dead as in repose, when, returning to their graves beyond the city gates with food and dainties, thou art wont to present offerings to thyself rather than to them; or when, coming from the graves again, thou art staggering under the effects of wine. But I want thy sober opinion. Thou callest the dead poor when thou speakest thine own thoughts, when thou art at a distance from them. For at their feast, where in a sense they are present and recline along with thee, it would never do to cast reproach upon their lot. Thou canst not but adulate those for whose sake thou art feasting it so sumptuously. Dost thou then speak of him as *poor* who feels not? How happens it that thou cursest, as one capable of suffering from thy curse, the man whose memory comes back on thee with the sting in it of some old injury? It is thine imprecation that "the earth may lie heavy on him," and that there may be trouble "to his ashes in the realm of the dead." In like manner, in thy kindly feeling to him to whom thou art indebted for favors, thou entreatest "repose to his bones and ashes," and thy desire is that among the dead he may "have pleasant rest." If thou hast no power of suffering after death, if no feeling remains,—if, in a word, severance from the body is the annihilation of thee, what makes thee lie against thyself, as if thou couldst suffer in another state? Nay, why dost thou fear death at all? There is nothing after death to be feared, if there is nothing to be felt. For though it may be said that death is dreadful not for anything it threatens afterwards, but because it deprives us of the good of life; yet, on the other hand, as it puts an end to life's discomforts, which are far more numerous, death's terrors are mitigated by a gain that more than outweighs the loss. And there is no occasion to be troubled about a loss of good things, which is amply made up for by so great a blessing as relief from every trouble. There is nothing dreadful in that which delivers from all that is to be dreaded. If thou shrinkest from giving up life because thy experience of it has been sweet, at any rate there is no need to be in any alarm about death if thou hast no knowledge that it is evil. Thy dread of it is the proof that thou art aware of its evil. Thou wouldst never think it evil—thou wouldst have no fear of it at all—if thou wert not sure that after it there is something to make it evil, and so a thing of terror. Let us leave unnoted at this time that natural way of fearing death. It is a poor thing for anyone to fear what is inevitable. I take up the other side, and argue on the ground of a joyful hope beyond our term of earthly life; for desire of posthumous fame is with almost every class an inborn thing. I have not time to speak of the Curtii, and the Reguli, or the brave men of Greece, who afford us innumerable cases of death despised for after renown. Who at this day is without the desire that he may be often remembered when he is dead? Who does not give all Endeavour to preserve his name by works of literature, or by the simple glory of his virtues, or by the splendor even of his tomb? How is it the nature of the soul to have these posthumous ambitions and with such amazing effort to prepare the things it can only use after decease? It would care nothing about the future, if the future were quite unknown to it. But perhaps thou thinkest thyself surer, after thy exit from the body, of continuing still to feel, than of any future resurrection, which is a doctrine laid at our door as one of our presumptuous suppositions. But it is also the doctrine of the soul; for if any one inquires about a person lately dead as though he were alive, it occurs at once to say, "He has gone." He is expected to return, then.

Chapter V.

These testimonies of the soul are simple as true, commonplace as simple, universal as commonplace, natural as universal, divine as natural. I don't think they can appear frivolous or feeble to any one, if he reflect on the majesty of nature, from which the soul derives its authority. If you acknowledge the authority of the mistress, you will own it also in the disciple. Well, nature is the mistress here, and her disciple is the soul. But everything the one has taught or the other learned, has come from God—the Teacher of the teacher. And what the soul may know from the teachings of its chief instructor, thou canst judge from that which is within thee. Think of that which enables thee to think; reflect on that which in forebodings is the prophet, the augur in omens, the foreseer of coming events. Is it a wonderful thing, if, being the gift of God to man, it knows how to divine? Is it anything very strange, if it knows the God by whom it was bestowed? Even fallen as it is, the victim of the great adversary's machinations, it does not forget its Creator, His goodness and law, and the final end both of itself and of its foe. Is it singular then, if, divine in its origin, its revelations agree with the knowledge God has given to His own people? But he who does not regard those outbursts of the soul as the teaching of a congenital nature and the secret deposit of an inborn knowledge, will say that the habit and, so to say, the vice of speaking in this way has been acquired and confirmed from the opinions of published books widely spread among men. Unquestionably the soul existed before letters, and speech before books, and ideas before the writing of them, and man himself before the poet and philosopher. Is it then to be believed, that before literature and its publication no utterances of the sort we have pointed out came from the lips of men? Did nobody speak of God and His goodness, nobody of death, nobody of the dead? Speech went a-begging, I suppose; nay, (the subjects being still awanting, without which it cannot even exist at this day, when it is so much more copious, and rich, and wise), it could not exist at all if the things which are now so easily suggested, that cling to us so constantly, that are so very near to us, that are somehow born on our very lips, had no existence in ancient times, before letters had any existence in the world—before there was a Mercury, I think, at all. And whence was it, I pray, that letters themselves came to know, and to disseminate for the use of speech, what no mind had ever conceived, or tongue put forth, or ear taken in? But, clearly, since the Scriptures of God, whether belonging to Christians or to Jews, into whose olive tree we have been grafted—are much more ancient than any secular literature, (or, let us only say, are of a somewhat earlier date, as we have shown in its proper place when proving their trustworthiness); if the soul have taken these utterances from writings at all, we must believe it has taken them from ours, and not from yours, its instruction coming more naturally from the earlier than the later works. Which latter indeed waited for their own instruction from the former, and though we grant that light has come from you, still it has flowed from the first fountainhead originally; and we claim as entirely ours, all you may have taken from us and handed down. Since it is thus, it matters little whether the soul's knowledge was put into it by God or by His book. Why, then, O man, wilt thou maintain a view so groundless, as that those testimonies of the soul have gone forth from the mere human speculations of your literature, and got hardening of common use?

Chapter VI.

Believe, then, your own books, and as to our Scriptures so much the more believe writings which are divine, but in the witness of the soul itself give like confidence to Nature. Choose the one of these you observe to be the most faithful friend of truth. If your own writings are distrusted, neither God nor Nature lie. And if you would have faith in God and Nature, have faith in the soul; thus you will believe yourself. Certainly you value the soul as giving you your true greatness,—that to which you belong; which is all things to you; without which you can neither live nor die; on whose account you even put God away from you. Since, then, you fear to become a Christian, call the soul before you, and put her to the question. Why does she worship another? why name the name of God? Why does she speak of demons, when she means to denote spirits to be held accursed? Why does she make her protestations towards the heavens, and pronounce her ordinary execrations earthwards? Why does she render service in one place, in another invoke the Avenger? Why does she pass judgments on the dead? What Christian phrases are those she has got, though Christians she neither desires to see nor hear? Why has she either bestowed them on us, or received them from us? Why has she either taught us them, or learned them as our scholar? Regard with suspicion this accordance in words, while there is such difference in practice. It is utter folly—denying a universal nature—to ascribe this exclusively to our language and the Greek, which are regarded among us as so near akin. The soul is not a boon from heaven to Latins and Greeks alone. Man is the one name belonging to every nation upon earth: there is one soul and many tongues, one spirit and various sounds; every country has its own speech, but the subjects of speech are common to all. God is everywhere, and the goodness of God is everywhere; demons are everywhere, and the cursing of them is everywhere; the invocation of divine judgment is everywhere, death is everywhere, and the sense of death is everywhere, and all the world over is found the witness of the soul. There is not a soul of man that does not, from the light that is in itself, proclaim the very things we are not permitted to speak above our breath. Most justly, then, every soul is a culprit as well as a witness: in the measure that it testifies for truth, the guilt of error lies on it; and on the day of judgment it will stand before the courts of God, without a word to say. Thou proclaimedst God, O soul, but thou didst not seek to know Him: evil spirits were detested by thee, and yet they were the objects of thy adoration; the punishments of hell were foreseen by thee, but no care was taken to avoid them; thou hadst a savor of Christianity, and withal wert the persecutor of Christians.

Elucidations.

I.

(Recognition of the Supreme God, cap. ii., p. 176.)

The passage referred to in the note, begins thus in Jowett's rendering: "The Ruler of the Universe has ordered all things with a view to the preservation and perfection of the whole etc." So, in the same book: "Surely God must not be supposed to have a nature which he himself hates." Again: "Let us not, then, deem God inferior to human workmen, who in proportion to their skill finish and perfect their works...or that God, the wisest of beings, who is willing and able to extend his care to all things, etc." Now, it is a sublime plan which our author here takes up, (making only slight reference to the innumerable citations which were behind his apostrophe to the soul if anyone should dispute it) to bid the soul stand forth and confess its consciousness of God.

II.

(Dæmons, cap. vi. p. 176.)

Those who would pursue the subject of Demonology, which Tertullian opens in this admirable treatise, should follow it up in a writer whom Tertullian greatly influenced, in many particulars, even when he presents a remarkable contrast. The Ninth Book of the *City of God* is devoted to inquiries which throw considerable light on some of the startling sayings of our author as to the heathen systems, and their testimony to the Soul's Consciousness of God and of the great enemy of God and the inferior spirit of Evil.